I0493758

Embracing Universal Individualism

Art as a Spiritual Construct

By

Waseem Rahman

Art is not a work of passion but a life long journey

Copyright © 2013, by Waseem Rahman

For information regarding special discounts for bulk Purchases, please contact Amazon.

ISBN-13:978-0615837413
ISBN-10:   0615837417

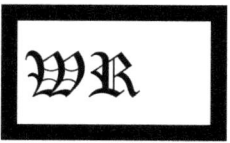

ACKNOWLEDGEMENTS

Art is not a work of passion but a life long journey.

This work is a product of my life experience in my personal life, in business and in the art world. It began when I was five years old as I was looking at English and Arabic Calligraphy as a part of my penmanship. I am grateful for the inspiration and brilliance of many calligraphers for the trans-generational source. The evolution of my art is derivative of these sources.

I am also very thankful to Carla Jankowski and Allen McNair from the Neighbourhood Writing Alliance, Journal of Ordinary Thought, the City of Chicago who all have critically looked at my work and given feedback and encouragement. My repertoire of material and arrangement has slowly evolved. It started to pervade the thoughts of those people who sincerely believed that this work is efficacious for the purpose which it is written.

For the production of this work, I wish to express my gratitude for everyone's kindness and their kind words.

---to Maryam & Fatima for their unconditional love

---to my brothers and to my sister in law, Rhonda, who have supported me through thick and thin.

---to my mother who is always there for me rain or shine.

---to my late father who always believed in me.

---to all the friends in the art world as well as in the business world

TABLE OF CONTENTS

    (a)Curve Movement
    (b)Outline
    (c)Contour Line
    (d)Organic Curve
    (e)Implied Lines and Curves

I. Introduction

A myriad of universal realities keeps humans engaged in soul-searching. We try to find the answers to questions like "Who I am?", "Where do I come from?", "What is the purpose of this life?", and "How does this superstructure called Universe run with such precision?"

Our endless curiosity helps us reveal the three dimensions of spirituality: the search for meaning in life, the search for a relationship with life's mysteries, and the search for the energy that would transform us to the next level of understanding about everything (Frankl, 1963; Paintner, 2007).

Initially we consider that there has to be something or someone who controls these dimensions, which leads us to sense the presence of divinity in everything. It makes us feel closer to the unknown, closer to our understanding of how the unknown works and closer to new insights into the becoming of things. This progression intensifies our inner drive to know, "What is the end?" Life, then, is a spiritual journey that addresses the individual and yet accommodates the universal. Those humans who engage themselves in a same spiritual pursuit of life adopt various paths to express their understanding about life and how it correlates with the greater universe.

From personal perspective, I find creativity is an intangible force residing within humans. It is transcendental in nature and challenges people to go beyond the ordinary range of human experience, understanding, and intelligence. The Sufi poet Rumi explains intelligence this way: there are (Barks & Moyne,

1997), two types of intelligence, one that is acquired from external learning and the other that resides within humans in a complete form. Rumi suggests that the second type of intelligence can be manifested by reflection upon certain spiritual truths and bringing out a new and broader comprehension of one's reality based on them. This also determines the spiritual sojourner's task: we must be a channel that expresses the fountainhead residing within us.

I, for one, have my canvas to become that channel and to share whatever I gathered in the course of my own spiritual journey.

I refine my spiritual quest by assimilating my own ideas with the knowledge that others have produced. These insights emanate from my background and evolve with my innate approach to ineffable art.

For example, I cannot explain the shifts in my artistic journey: why I was attracted to impressionistic and landscape works, then Islamic art and calligraphy, and finally, an abstract-style such as *CIRCUMLOCUISM*. All I know is that an inherent sense of choice has guided me on those occasions. I cannot accomplish anything without creating such a canvas and can achieve what I want to do when I become the performer in the creation of my art. In this way, I have grown an affinity to the universal agenda of spirituality, while developing a strong sense of individualism.

II. Correlation between Spirituality and Art

Art is the most ancient tool of human expression. Even before they reached the stage of organized verbal or written communication, people have used Art to understand and reveal their spiritual lives. As civilizations advanced and became more sophisticated humans started fusing all acquired knowledge into art.

For example, cuneiform is the earliest known form of written expression. It was developed in Sumer around 30 BC. Over time, humans improved cuneiform and laid the groundwork for the first alphabets. This process of transference could be easily shared and civilizations took such an approach to their works of art. Examples such as Egyptian hieroglyphics (Collier, 1998; Davis, 1987) inscribed on the pyramids, or the Islamic scriptures that adorn the walls of the 13th century Alhambra Palace in Spain (Ruggles, 1993) strongly support this view. So what drove the Egyptians to use hieroglyphs in the pyramids? Copious documents show that the governing philosophy of Islam has made the scripture its main tool for spiritual expression.

First, the real meaning of Islam, *Al-Tawhid*, denotes a metaphysical belief such as *Unity of Being*, which emphasizes the spiritual significance of the *Void*. Second, Islam does not see Allah (God) as an entity but as someone to be realized as the Supreme Creator of everything and we will be answerable to Him. Thus, Allah has been portrayed in an anthropomorphous form in the Holy Qur'an (The Word of Allah), and His divinity as well as the spirit of Islam is expressed through symbolic language (Hossein, 1987). Therefore, the Holy Qur'an is the source of every art-form in Islamic Art; a notion further consolidated by the fact that Qur'an recognizes pen and ink as the materials for depicting Allah's divinity (Saeed, 2011). Such practice thus shows a clear and deep connection between spirituality and art. Images created by an inner call actually mirror the authentic soul of a painter by expressing his/her deep experiences. I subscribe to Carl Jung's (Welch, 1982) view that such images provide clues to the unlived life and urge all to find and exploit such clues to their spiritual gain.

On the other hand, the painter also enjoys material gain as he/she passes through four stages of creativity, such as *preparation, incubation, illumination,* and *verification* (Graham, 1981), which actually makes art a spiritual practice, as it enables the painter to connect with his/her inner self. Therefore, it is not difficult to find that other points of view also corroborate the relationship between spirituality and art.

III. Interrelationship among Spirituality, Culture and Art

Though it is difficult to frame all nuances of interrelationship within spirituality, culture, and art in one's life, yet one can look back and gather the events that reflect such relationships. When I do the same I find the ambience of learning at my home, the education I received in my life, the experiences I gathered from the professional world, and the social circles I belong to, all contain such reflections. I was attracted to calligraphy by the culture of my homeland, and since calligraphy connects both the Islamic concept of spirituality and the concept of art, it started playing the role of catalyst in shaping my perceptions regarding spirituality and art. In the process, I developed an intrinsic desire to perfect the flow of energy and rhythmic movement in my handwriting. That, in turn, helped me shape my idea of spirituality and express it through my art.

Similarly, my academic, social, and professional circles helped me gather ideas about other theoretical concepts of art. I found the cubist movement (Cooper, 1995) interesting, especially its idea of capturing different realities within a single work of art. At the same time, I had come across Kandinsky's (1977) paintings and the spiritual philosophy that guided them. Thus it would not be wrong to say that cubism and Kandinsky's art inspired my thoughts about the relationship between an individual and the universe.

First, the cubists' penchant for depicting multiple realities within a still-life frame made me aware of the impact of space-time has on what we perceive as reality. This in turn prompted me to ponder how space-time affected cubism too since at its inception in 1906 in Paris. I wondered whether the African masks extensively used by cubists, especially by Picasso, or the violin (a symbol of pathos) used by many of these artists conveyed the message of an impending disaster. My spiritual self suddenly pointed to the futility of material desire and suggested looking beyond that. Such a disaster in recent history was the collapse of the global financial market in 2008. People were applying themselves to acquiring material riches instead of providing any real service to mankind. The tremor of the collapse still reverberates around the globe.

Such a state of introspection eventually sparked a new idea: that we are missing the big picture. We are ignoring its projection in our lives, where a universal oneness that encompasses all elements keeps intact the individual identities of each element. It appeared to me as if a little dot – a singularity -- may be sufficient to interpret individualism as well as the universe, think Big

Bang Theory. In fact, the same patterns and traits do take place at all levels of the cosmos, ranging from the smallest particle to the entire universe. Did that transform my worldview? Had I emerged from a new plane of thought? Was it the impact of space-time on my reality and me? Answering the above queries gave birth to a new realization; I am working with the cosmology of the curve and circular movement. I will be a channel to express the fountainhead residing within me.

However, it would be wrong to assume that I have all along been representing my 40 years of spiritual journey through my art. On the contrary, I was completely absorbed with my business world, until I woke up to my spiritual world. In fact, I did not exult in the fact that my compulsory calm changed my life when I slipped into my artistic robe.

IV. The Cosmology of Curve and Circular Movement

The idea of *CIRCUMLOCUISM* emanated from my spiritual and metaphysical center. However, it is not a concept that disregards the legacy of art, nor does it defy the contemporary world and the world of modern art. It just aims to attract people who want to look beyond the beauties of mere circular motion depicted in my works and to delve deep in the vast, symbolic phantasmagorical reality of a spiritual journey through life.

CIRCUMLOCUISM is an expression of art that goes beyond every-day comprehension. The artistic movements under this concept identify the range of all possible experiences both on the micro and macro levels in the movement of lines. Alongside, the curves in such an art are capable of defining an edge of a form or create an optical illusion of mass in their patterns or volume.

The process of my creation involves a unique art form defined by the curves that contain spiritual and mystical expression. To create the same I had to invent a special paintbrush to work on a flat surface. I paint in one continuous motion across my canvas. The brush never leaves the canvas until I complete the image I wish to create with known and unknown direction. The content may vary to some extent, but my artworks mostly contain what we experience and observe in the moving universe, where trillions and quadrillions of transactions are happening at the same time. For example, in my painting I represent the dark matter of the universe as it bends the light of the stars in white curvilinear lines across a black canvas.

Kandinsky (1977) suggests that the color black represents death. It may sound depressing initially, but if we look through the new windows of our perception, we realize that death does not end our spiritual journey. Just as the dark matter in the celestial realm acts as the means to provide an opening for the universe to hold itself together, similarly the color black represents a material opening at the gate for man's experience of spirituality.

I prefer expressing my art with material objects, such as the color black, which I find spiritual and mystical in nature when comparing it with the dark matter of the universe. In the realm of space, dark matter could not have purpose without the existence of the celestial bodies, nor could the universe exist in its present form without the influence of dark matter.

Back on earth, the "dark matter" of suffering serves the purpose of our own growth. This does not mean that we should seek to suffer, but when suffering comes, it directs us to change those behaviors that promote our suffering. Suffering prompts us to change our negative behaviors, so I have learned from my own life experience.

Kandinsky's (1977) pyramid expresses of the spiritual development of various artists. An artist's growth reaches a point that connotes the ultimate expression of that artist. Each side of the pyramid reflects one aspect of reality:

1) Material reality

2) Spiritual reality

Material reality expresses itself through the dimension of time as an action that has a beginning, middle, and an end. Spiritual realization, on the other hand, takes no time to manifest in one's consciousness. It takes human knowledge to discover material reality; it takes faith to acquire spiritual reality. However, Kandinsky's pyramid for the spiritual development of the artist is imperfect in its representation of man's reality. It is a manmade structure rather than a spiritual tool. We can better understand His essence if we think of the one Creator as expressing Himself in two aspects of reality (Faith/Knowledge; Spiritual/Material; Space/Time; No Time Required/Time Required).-

DIVINE has two aspects:

Faith	Knowledge
Spiritual	Material
Space	Time
No time required	Time element required

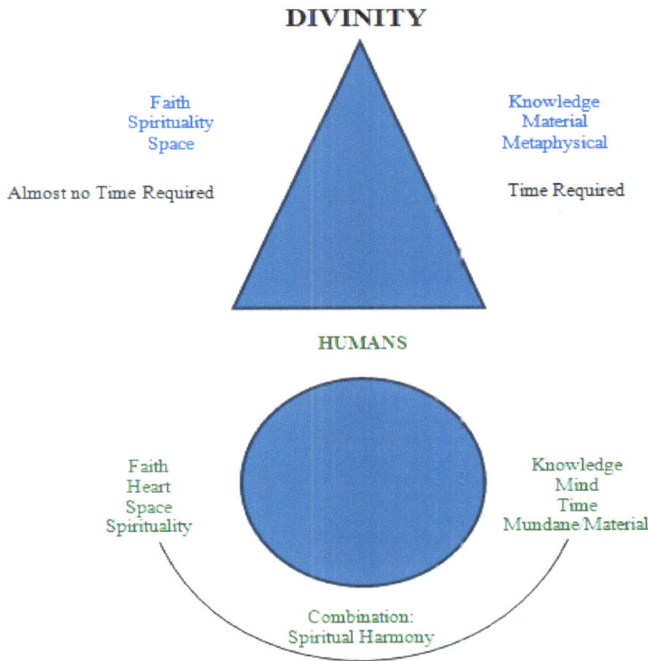

DIVINITY

Faith
Spirituality
Space

Almost no Time Required

Knowledge
Material
Metaphysical

Time Required

HUMANS

Faith
Heart
Space
Spirituality

Knowledge
Mind
Time
Mundane Material

Combination:
Spiritual Harmony

Figure 1
Figure 1: Framework of Material and Spiritual

Reality

When we use the curve as a model, we experience the unity inherent in both the material and spiritual reality of human existence. This observation provides a sufficient hint that a curve is an appropriate model of the universe and man in the expression of abstract art today. As the microcosm of the atom and the macrocosm of the celestial worlds reflect the model of the curve, the spiritual unity of humankind takes the middle ground of physical existence.

When we see how a curve progresses in an abstract piece of art, we encounter the progress of both the divine and mundane or material in our world. At this point, I believe that spiritual harmony or balance can result from the mere act of viewing one of my paintings.

V. Defining Line Movements:

I start my art moving with a dot. I let it move in any direction suggested by my heart and mind, until it becomes a thin or dash line. As the line moves forward like the ripples of a wave, it curves to move in a different or unknown direction. As we pass through the unknown zone, it suddenly intersects another path or line, or reality, whether happy or sad before crossing over and continuing its journey to its next destination. This continuous movement may zigzag different lines at different intervals until they reach their final destination. The whole expression reminds us that all journeys end at a point of time; be it our lives on this earth, or the galaxies in the cosmos, or even the universe itself, where the journey leaves a footprint, which time would impact again.

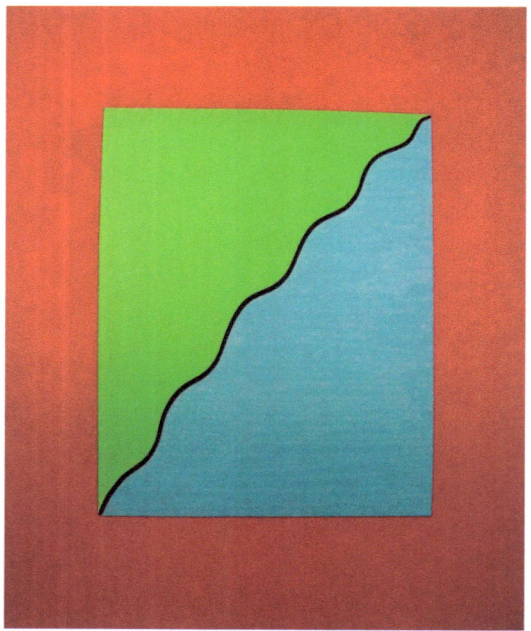

Figure 1: Curve Movement

(a) Curve Movement

Geometric lines are the byproducts or subsets of the circular or curve movement. Evenly rendered geometric lines (e.g. a pyramid and sections of straight or horizontal lines) may appear straight lines but in reality are circular or curved as we find them at the subatomic level or at the cosmological level. With circular motion, these lines would create different shapes or a myriad of realities, as we find when the circular movements cross each other. We live in the time of reason and knowledge. Reason is God's greatest gift to humans. There would not be any humans without the reasoning capacity. Therefore, it is not difficult to consider balanced and circular or curve shapes to represent rationality and the intellectual mind. Even the Neoclassical painters understood the aesthetics of the Greeks and composed their paintings with straight lines and curves. We find examples of the same in the works of Jacques-Louis David's treatment of the arches in his famous paintings such as *The Death of Marat* (Neo-Classicism, 2012a) and The *Death of Horatii* (Neo-Classicism, 2012b).

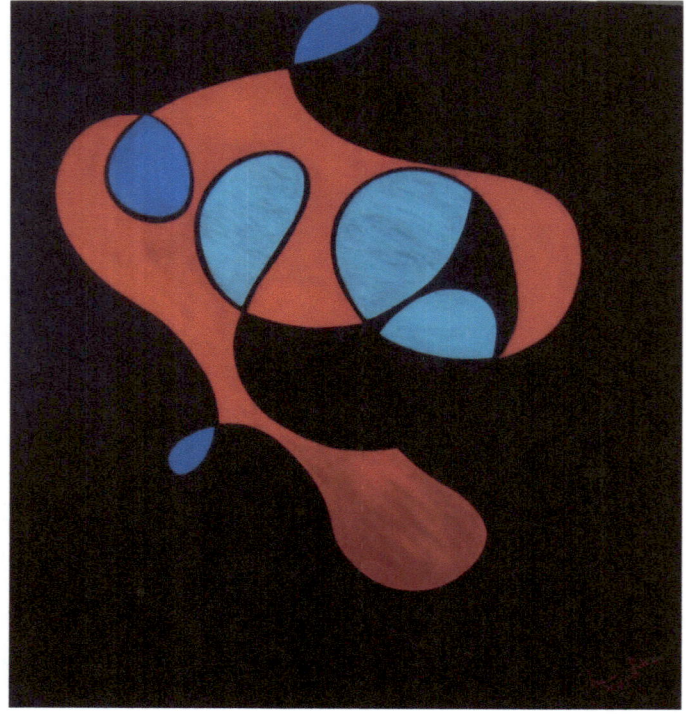

Figure 2: Outline

(b) *Outline*

In my composition, the outline is used to

create shapes that lead to different realities. The

line represents a journey that has a beginning and

an end, just like the realities of space-time. The

outline could be thick and may vary in width. It

can be as thin as a pencil line or black on black,

which is usually invisible to the naked eye if one

looks only at the composition. However, seen

under a very bright light, one can see lines have a

flattening effect. Lines here symbolically

represent the realities of human existence, while

the line curves represent the edge of a shape and

create an optical illusion of mass in their patterns

or volume.

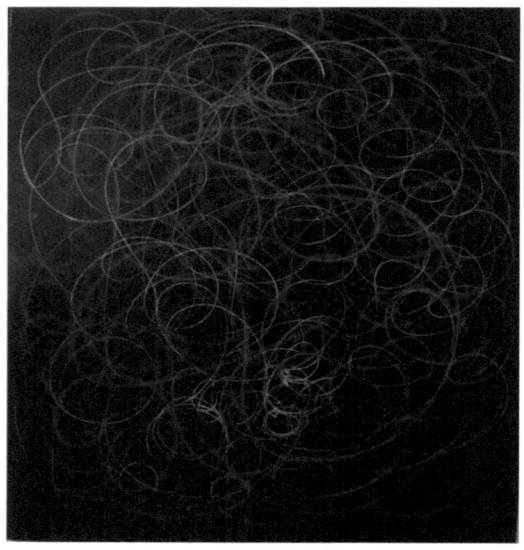

Figure 3: Contour Line

(c) Contour Line

A contour line follows the edge of a curvature shape. This results in a three-dimensional effect. The light can create this illusion by getting darker where there is shadow and lighter where there is less shadow. I took a page from the works of Ingres (1780-1867), whom many consider as the master of the contour line (Artble, 2012).

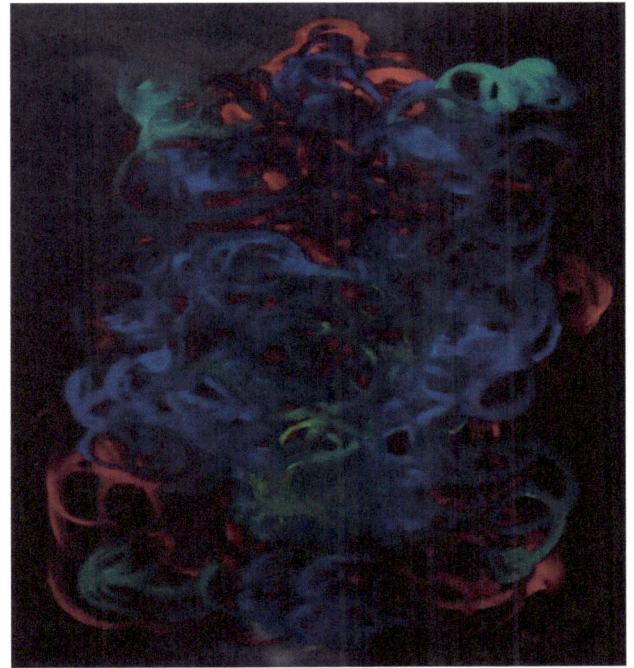

Figure 4: Organic Curves

(d) Organic Curves

Organic curved lines help create real

shapes in the every-day world and the cosmos.

For example, using circles or curve movement to

give a real sense of belonging evokes a common

saying, "the world is round". Curves remind us

that everything ultimately comes back to the original form. The use of curved lines is the natural progression, as they can represent many different realities and things, such as the realities of human existence or galaxies in the universe. . For example, when a supernova explodes, it gives amazing colors of different gases and these gases eventually contribute to the creation of new stars. One can easily draw a parallel to the variety in microscopic cells or atoms with the variety in man, besides recalling string theory, which attempts to unify the forces (including gravity) by representing particles as different modes of underlying building blocks, the strings.

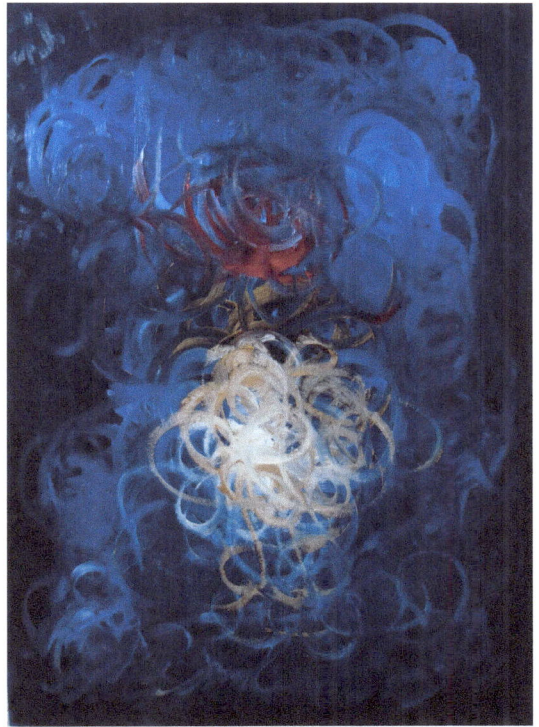

Figure 5: Implied Lines and Curves

(e) Implied Lines and Curves

In my composition, I explicitly draw or paint curved lines. I imply arrangements of shapes by lines crossing each other to create different realities. This practice may have a distant resemblance with the artwork of others.

Vincent Van Gogh's *"The Starry Night"* (1889) is an example. He too used curved lines to illuminate the color and shape of the sky. He arranged the movement of the clouds and curved the almost circular lines of the moon and the stars to create a centrifugal movement around the central image of the painting.

He also depicted the stress and tumult of the moment by placing the curved lines above the tranquil homes.

VI. Elements of Art

Element 1: [.]

The dot placed between the brackets is the metaphoric start or birth of an art. It also represents the occurrences such as the birth of a child, a star, a galaxy, or our physical and spiritual existence.

Element 2: [——]

The line placed between the brackets represents the starting point of a journey or an exploration of oneself, such as a journey of one's life. It may also represent the formation of a star or a galaxy or the other realms of reality.

Element 3: [$\propto$]

The curve placed between the brackets represents the turns or shifts of human life, where the course of life often directs us towards different destinations. Alongside, the curve also represents the drastic change in a person's mental state caused by the loss of dear ones or a reversal of fortune (the U-turn), besides representing the steps of formation and growth of a galaxy, an atom, or of a person.

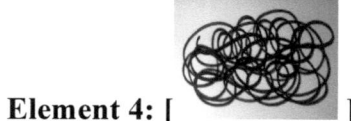

Element 4: [**]**

The example of a *line moving in various curves* placed within the above bracket represent all intersections faced in a journey, be it a journey of a human life or a journey of a star in the galaxy. At the same time, these lines also

represent the meeting and separation of elements

in a journey, like a person moving away from his

friends or his family or returning to them.

Altogether, intersections in this case highlight all

the transactions found in life as well as in this

universe.

Element 5: [OOOOOOO]

Colors comprise of the fifth element of art.

Colors are the laws of attraction which are

embedded in our spiritual and material world.

They represent the beauty in one's

experience and stimuli to uplift the human soul.

VII. Conclusion

Emergence of the Concept of Universal Individualism

Two points emerge in the course of my artistic journey: all elements of this universe are connected with one another and all journeys have a beginning, middle and an end.

The first point highlights the fact that just like the state of relationship between atoms at a microscopic level of existence, there is a connection between two separate electrons if the properties match regardless of the distance between them. What I interpret from the above view is that both the universe and the individual are equally important in terms of relationship.

Second, that all humans and atoms possess the same characteristics such as a beginning and an end. We can infer that all individualism is universal in its basic nature.

From the above findings, I can infer that *CIRCUMLOCUISM* emanates from universal individualism, where the curves as well as the colors contain equal value while embracing the canvas that serves as the universe. I believe that the more people embrace universal individualism, the more there will be peace and prosperity. People will realize that all wars for dominance and material gains are futile. They will see that such gains do not increase the potential value of any human.

VIII. For Further Consideration

These Are Some Of The Salient Features of My Art:

Five features have great bearing on my art:

1. A strong presence of the concept of a beginning, middle and an end, which involves

   i. Its creation

   ii. The viewer's perception of it

   iii. The intellectual and the emotional conclusion drawn by a person from it

2. The influence of the current social environment, where there is a lack of individual experience of the innate

harmony between one's spiritual

world and material world

3. An honest attempt to influence people

who seek spiritual harmony

4. Expression of the above harmony

through the curvilinear nature of this

art.

5. Presence of elements that can act as

catalysts to the construction of

spiritual harmony.

IX. Final Observation:

The rapid growth in information

technology is contributing new knowledge

regarding the relationships among elements,

which I feel will gradually enhance the human

understanding of both the mundane and spiritual

nature of reality. Such a state of affairs would be

more conducive to decipher the statements placed

in my work. That apart, I still feel that we are only

a few steps away from understanding the

mechanism of the divinity. I am sure that I will

achieve that, having already realized that life is

one wonderful spiritual journey.

Some Abstracts and their Possible Interpretation:

Let me share some possible interpretations

of the following works of mine:

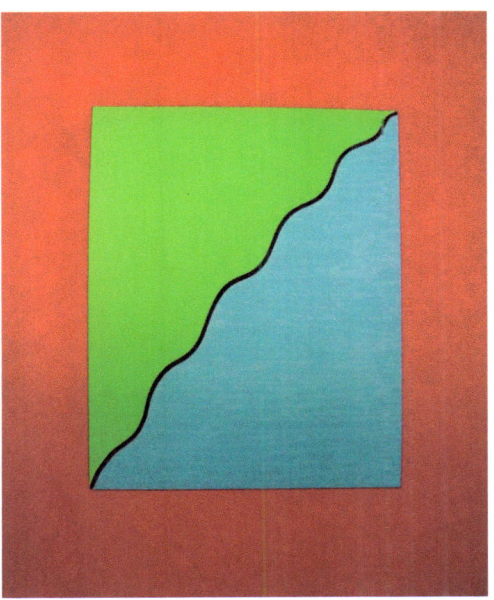

Picture 1: Red, Green and Blue

This painting contains a simple line

drawing to depict the separation of physical

reality and spiritual reality. Although the field of red interrupts the continuity of the waving line, the viewer can imagine that the line is in fact infinite in its influence on the structure of both the green space and the blue. The red engulfs the other three colors. This also translates to different interpretation.

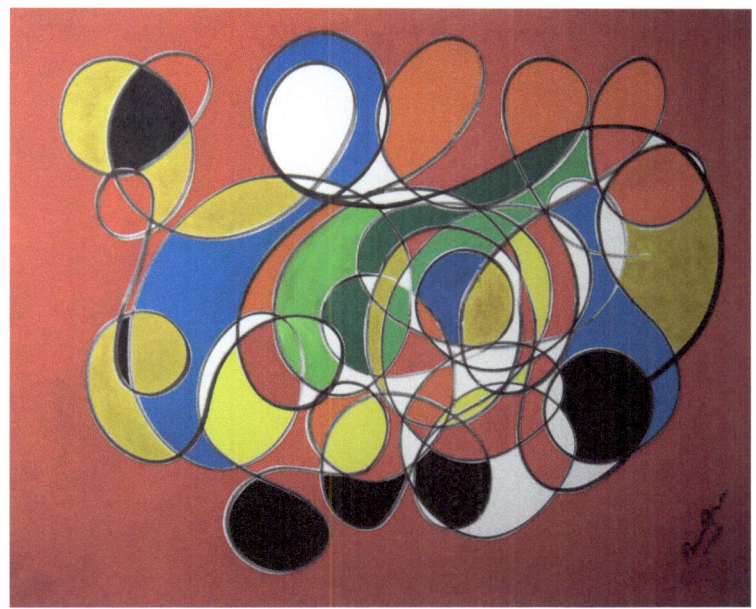

Picture 3: Manifestation

This picture contains an intensely lit background to reflect the dynamism of the cosmos. While representing the speed of an atom traveling through physical space, it also displays myriad possibilities in the subatomic and celestial realms and the multiplicity of shapes. The dominance of the color red symbolizes the warmth of the state at the time of manifestation of an element. This picture depicts the harmonious state that occurs at the time of manifestation of any element; much in the mold of a flower that blooms or when a child first learns to walk, or when a painter suddenly receives a new light of realization.

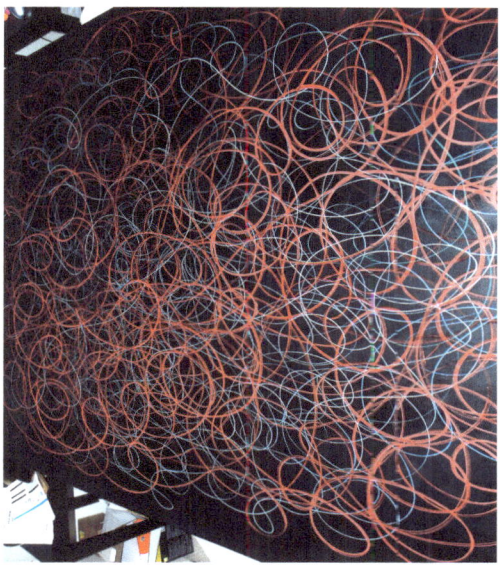

Picture 4:

This is one of the most complex works of my art. It depicts how the universe transcends all thought and activity. The movement of the curved lines in this work captures the dynamism of motion, and engages the primary sense of sight. It invites the viewers to engage themselves in comprehending the ultimate reality and true spirituality.

References

Artble. (2012). Jean Auguste Dominique Ingres. Retrieved November 15, 2012, from http://www.artble.com/artists/jean_auguste_dominique_ingres

Barks, C. & Moyne, J. (1997). *The essential Rumi.* Edison, NJ: Castle Books.

Collier, M. & Manley, B. (1998). *How to read Egyptian hieroglyphs: A step-by step guide to teach yourself.* British Museum Press.

Cooper, D. (1995). *The Cubist Epoch.* NY: Phaidon Press.

Davis, W.V. (1987). *Reading the past: Egyptian hieroglyphics.* British Museum Press.

Frankl, V.E. (1963). Man's search for meaning. NY: Harper Collins.

Graham, W. (1981). Stages in the creative process. In (A. Rothenberg & C.R. Hausman eds.), *The Creativity Question* (pp. 69-73). NC: Duke University Press.

Hossein, N.S. (1987). *Islamic art and spirituality.* Ipriwich, Suffolk: Golgon Press.

Kandinsky, W. (1977). *Concerning the spiritual art.* Dover Publications.

Neo-Classicism. (2012a). Retrieved November 15, 2012, from
http://www.bc.edu/bc_org/avp/cas/his/CoreArt/art/neocl_dav_marat.html

Neo-Classicism. (2012b). Retrieved November 15, 2012, from
http://www.bc.edu/bc_org/avp/cas/his/CoreArt/art/neocl_dav_oath.html

Paintner, C.V. (2007). The relationship between spirituality and artistic expression: Cultivating the capacity for imaging. *Spirituality in Higher Education,* 3(2):1-6

Ruggles, D. F. (1993). Arabic Poetry and Architectural Memory in Al-Andalus. *Arts Orientalis,* 23: 171-178.

Saeed, K.M. (2011). Islamic art and its spiritual message. *International Journal of Humanities and Social Science,* 1(2): 227-234.

Welch, J. (1982). *Spiritual pilgrims: Carl Jung and Theresa of Alivia.* NY: Paulist Press.

`

INDEX

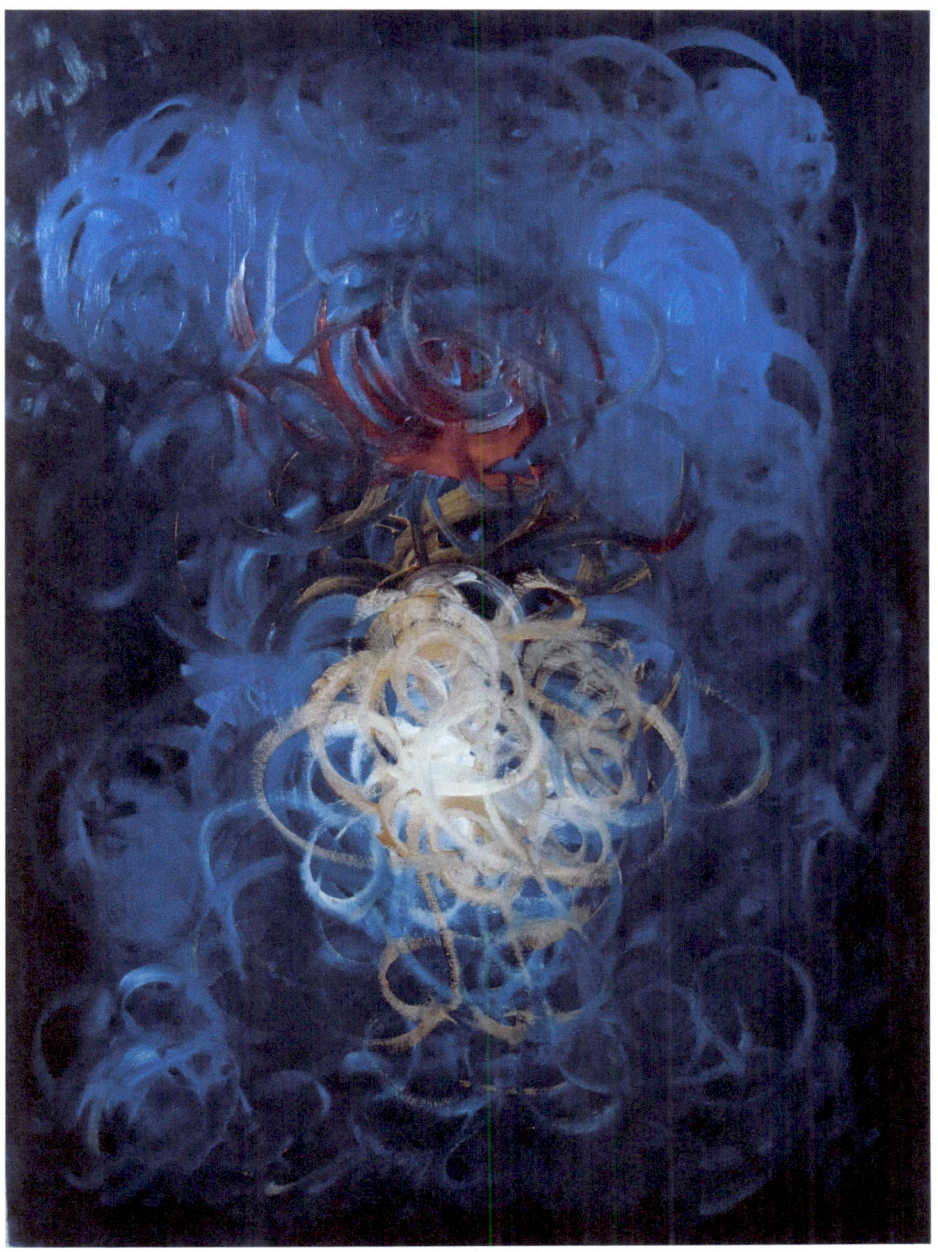

BLUE 48X36

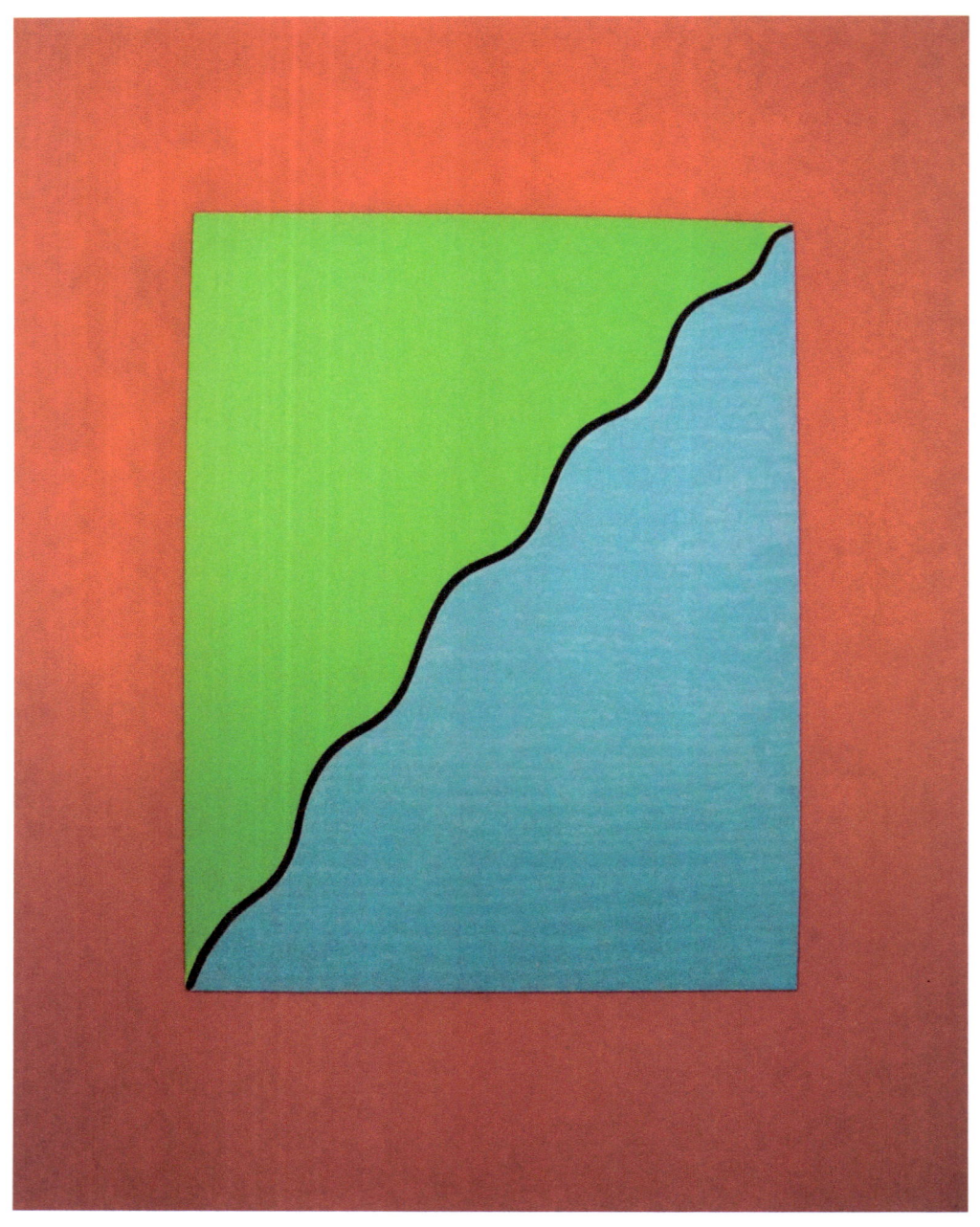

C P& US 60X48

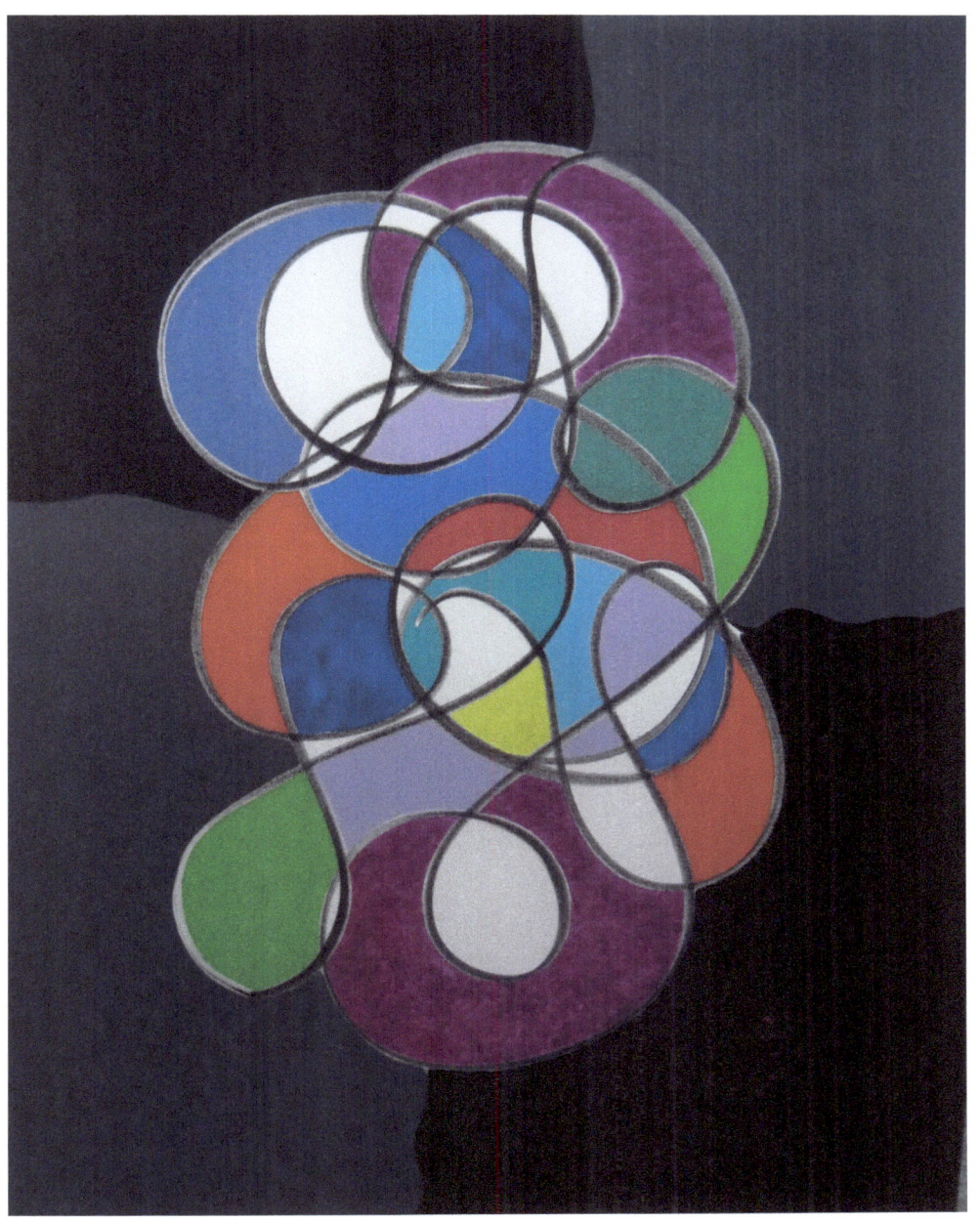

UNTITLED 48X36

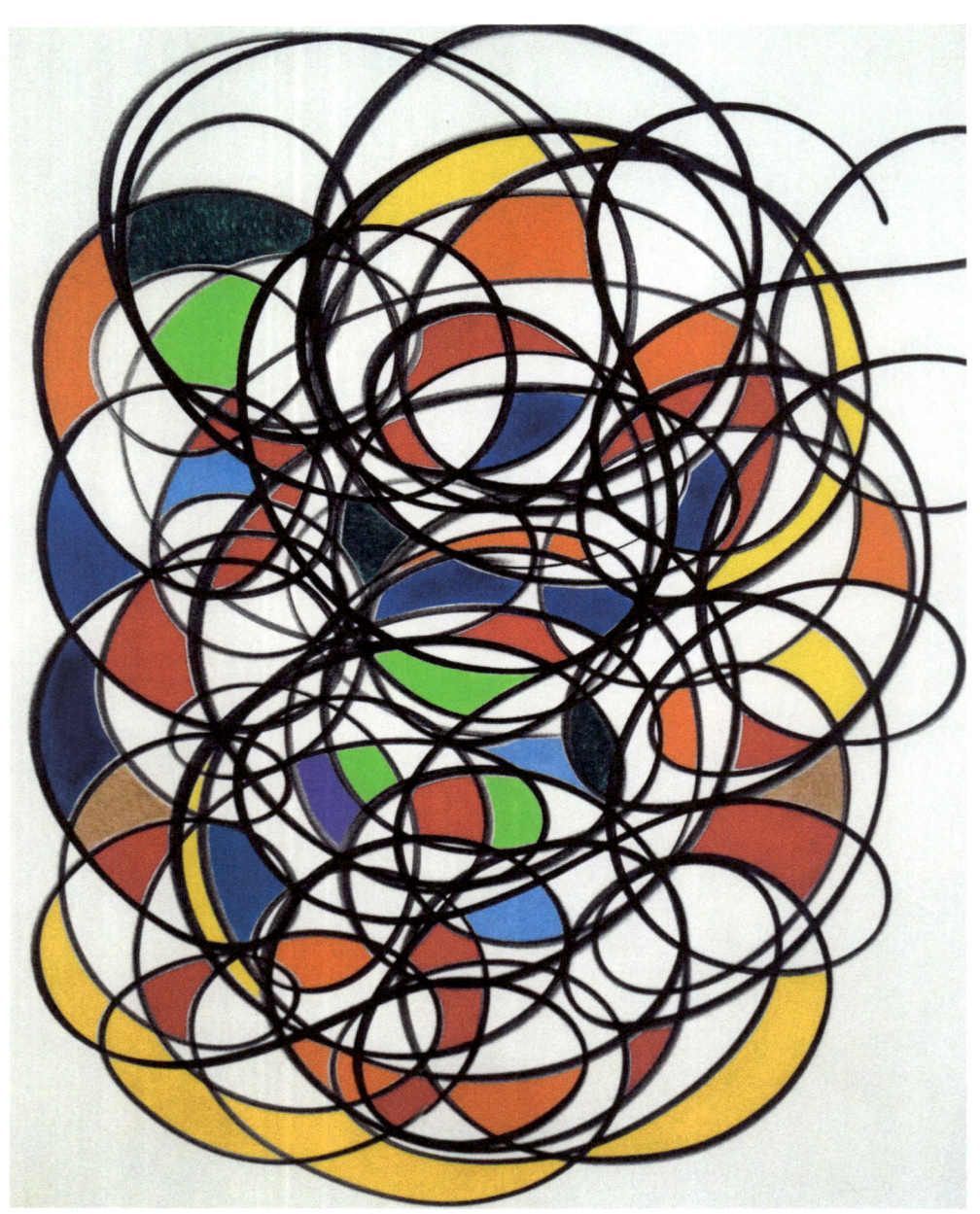

UNIVERSAL HARMONY 48X36

THE BIRTH 48X36

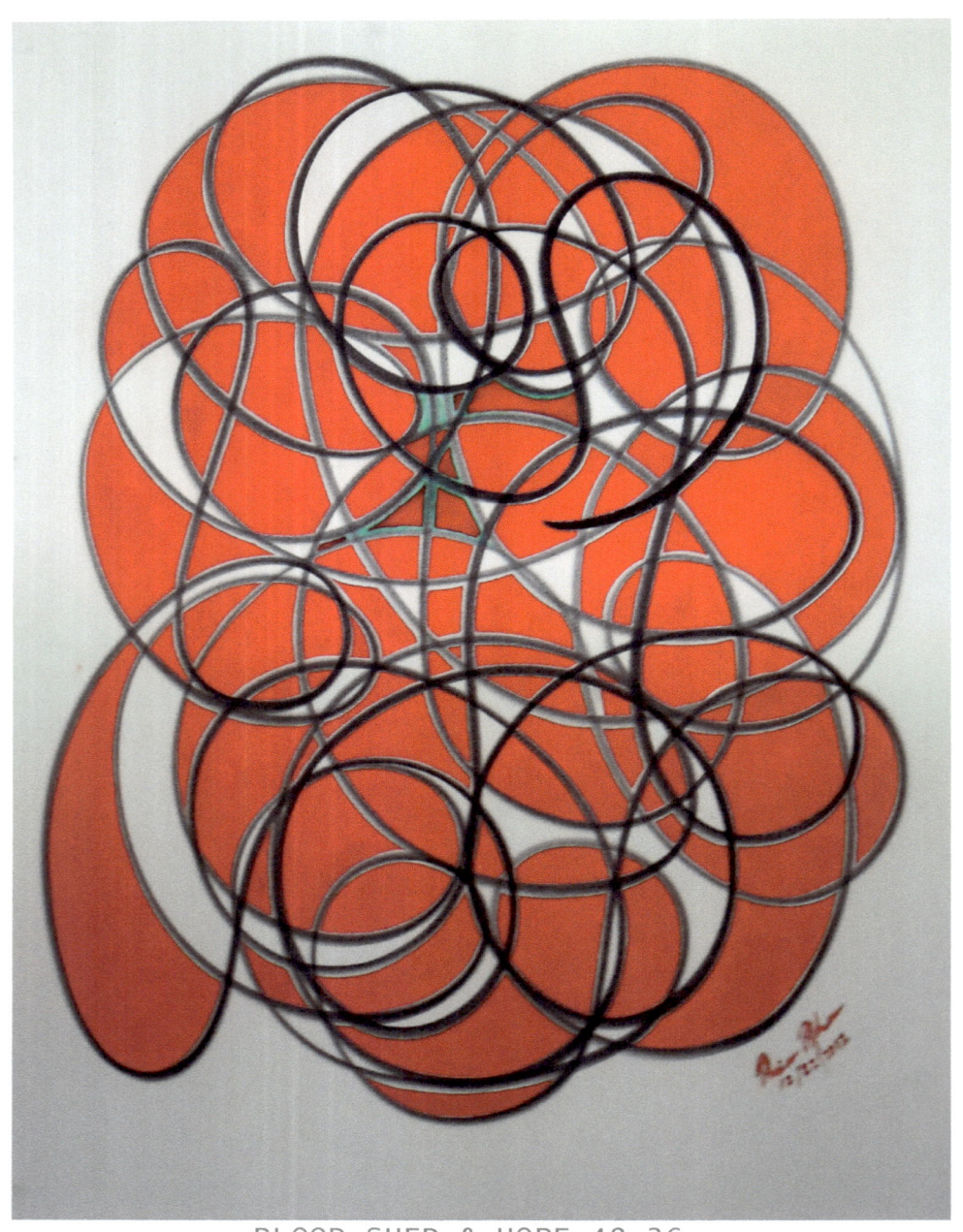

BLOOD SHED & HOPE 48x36

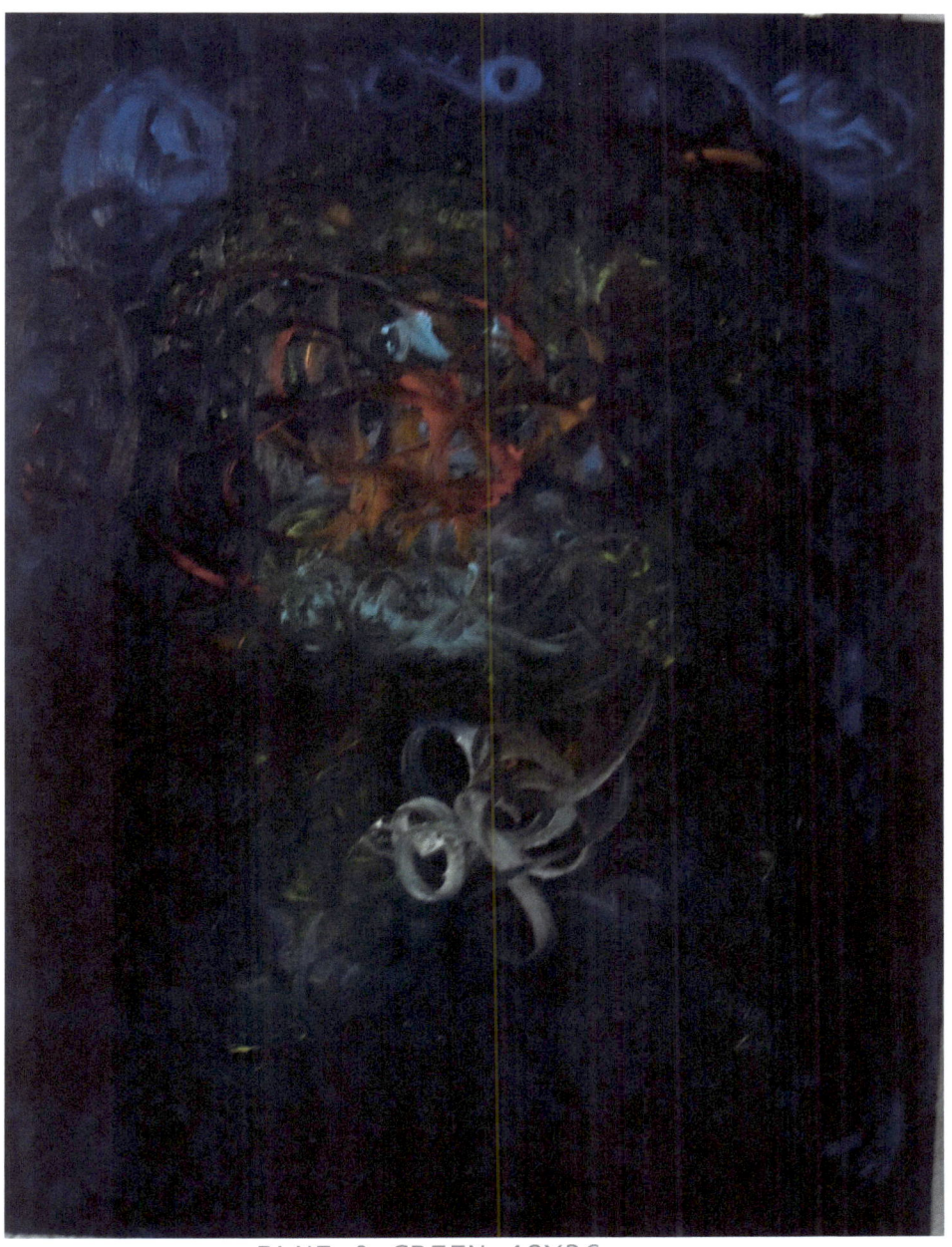

BLUE & GREEN 48X36

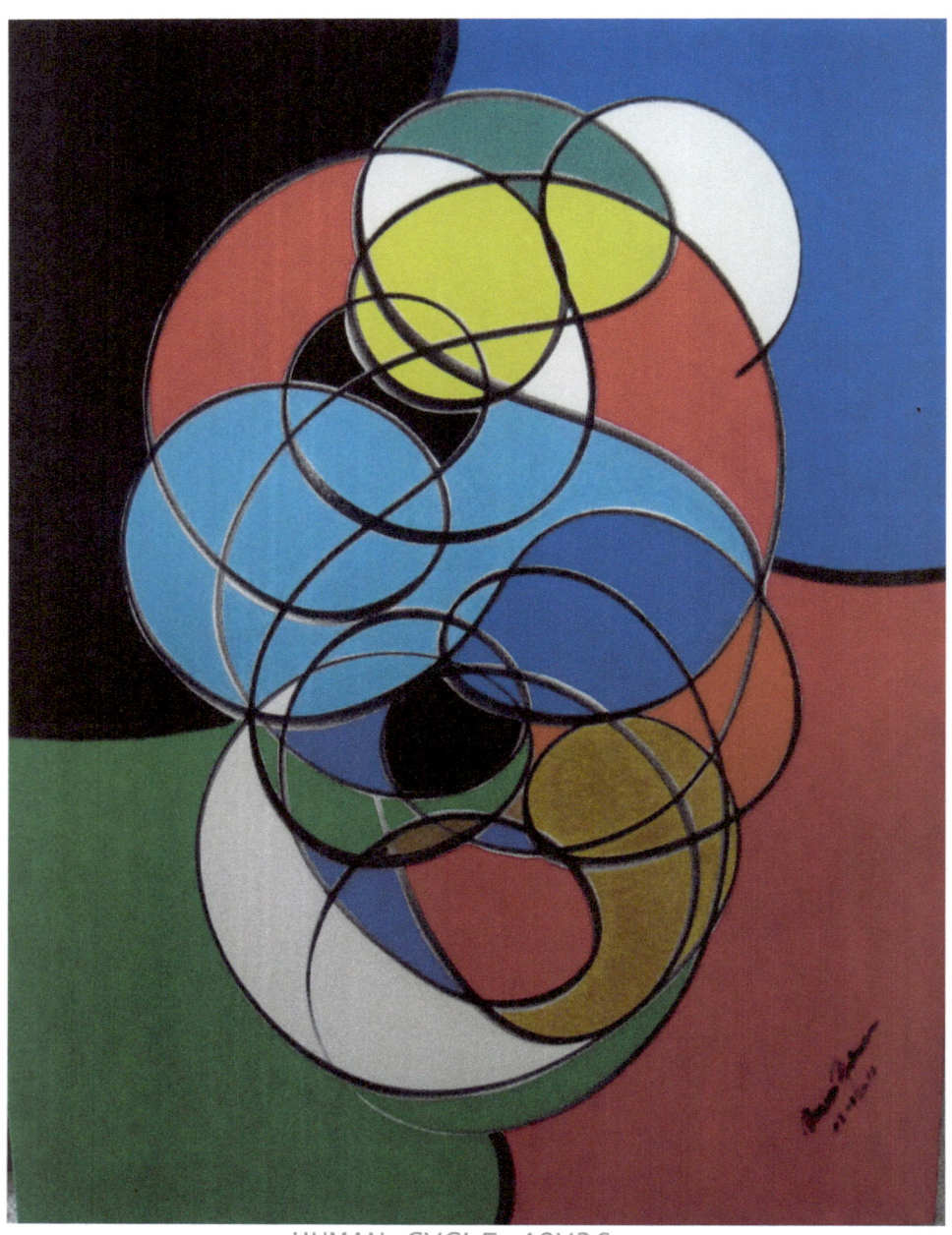

HUMAN CYCLE 48X36

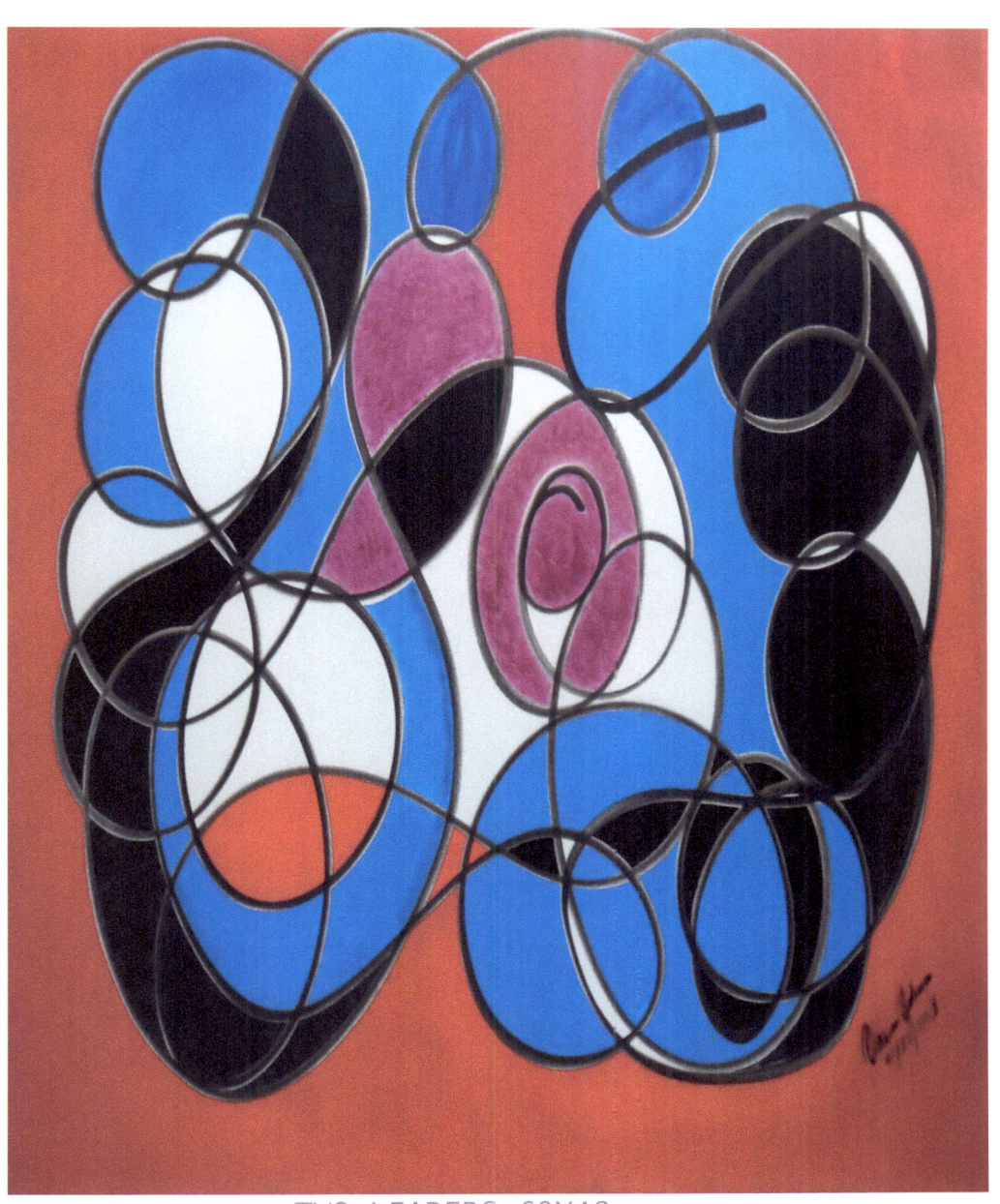

TWO LEADERS 60X48

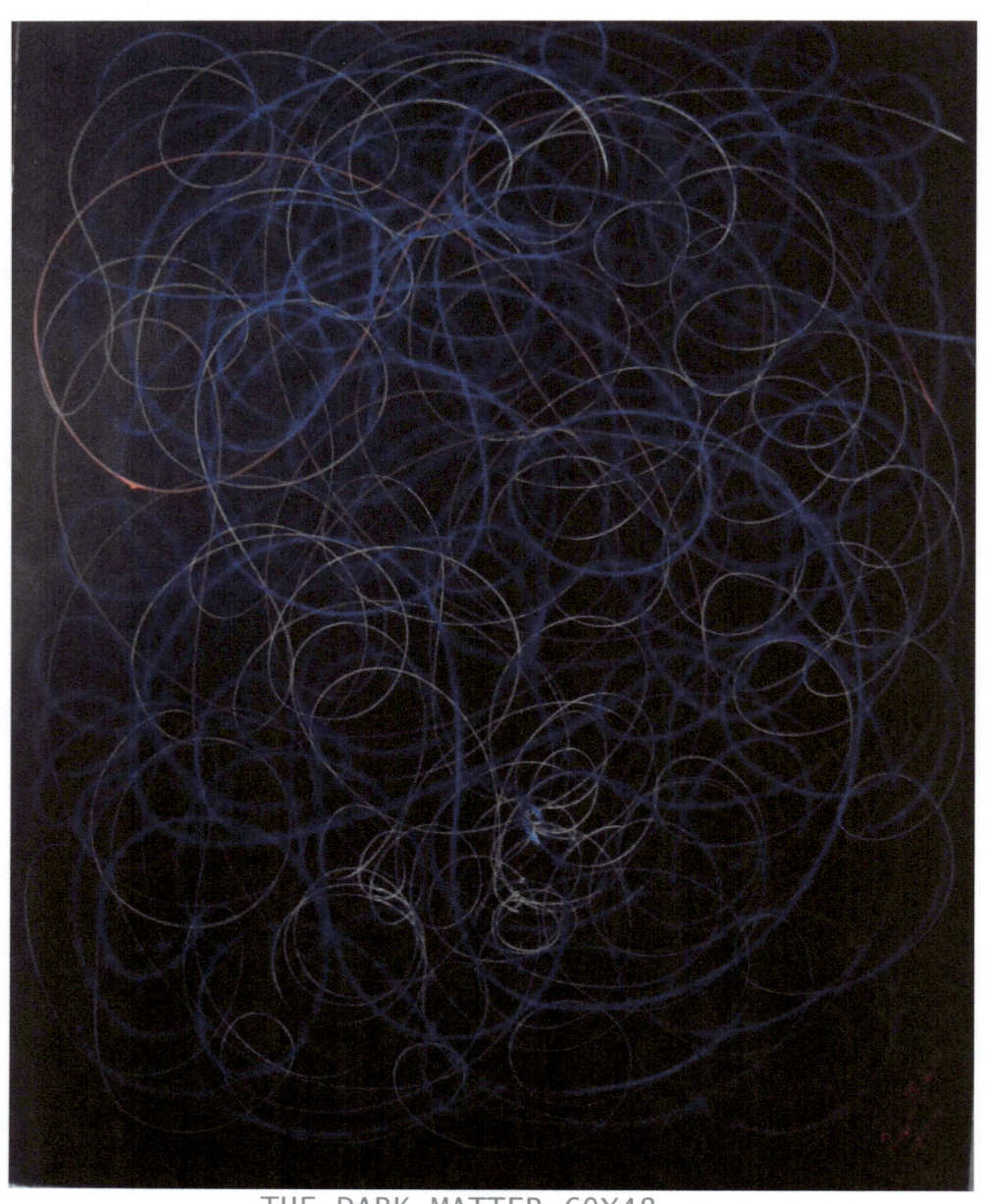

THE DARK MATTER 60X48

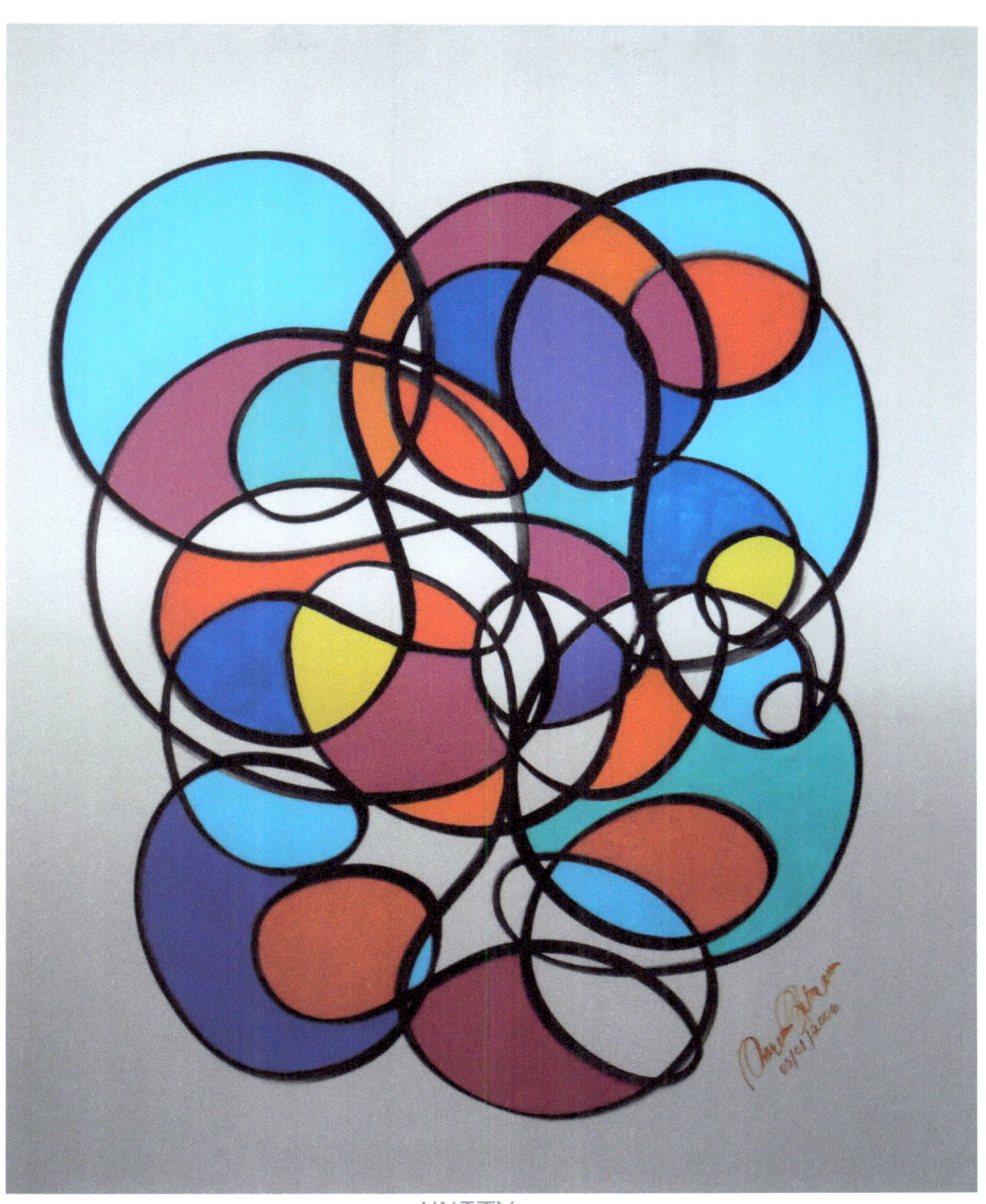

UNITY

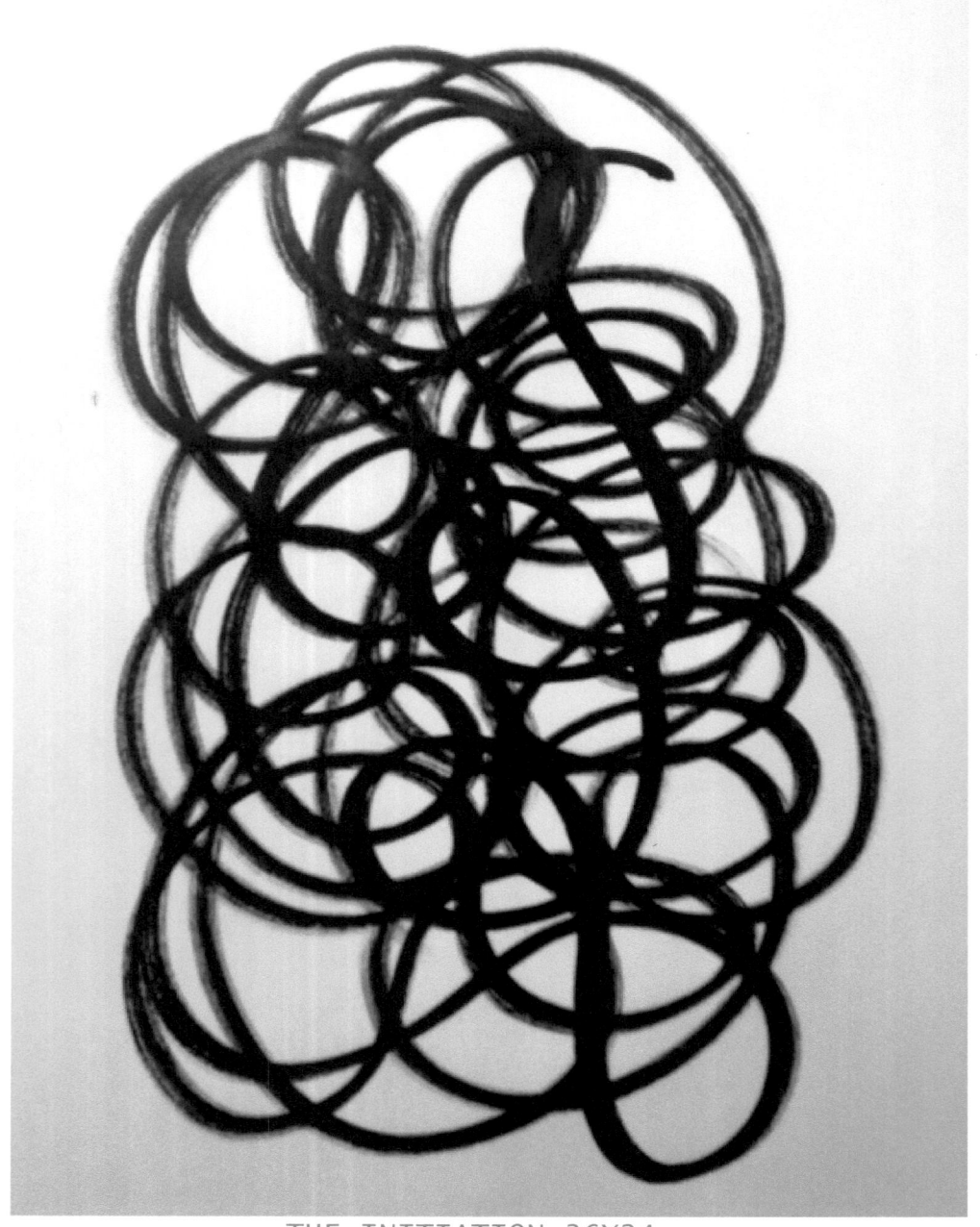

THE INITIATION 36X24

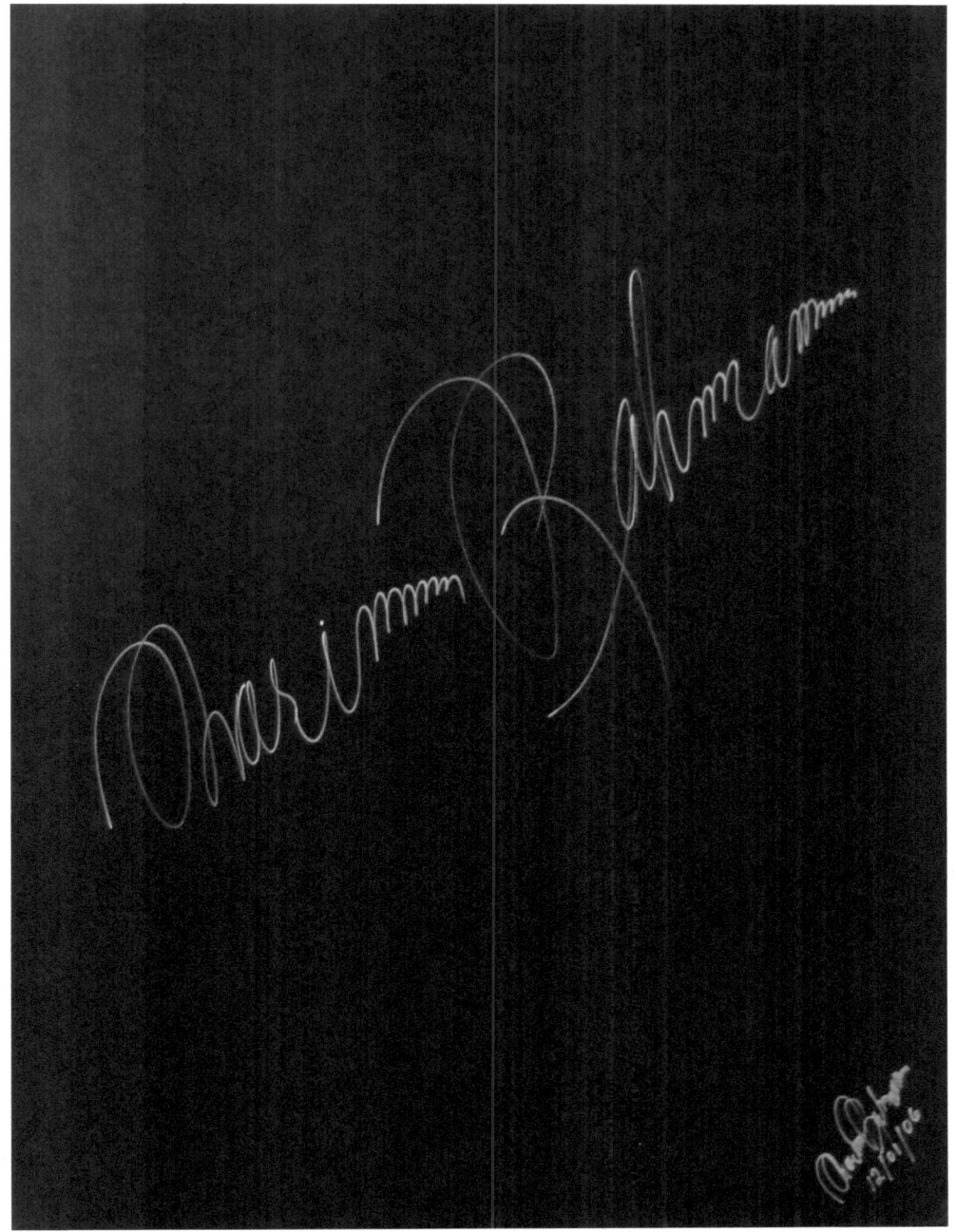

THE FOUNDATION 48X36